Red Fields

POEMS FROM IRAQ

Red Fields

POEMS FROM IRAQ

JASON POUDRIER

MONGREL EMPIRE PRESS
NORMAN, OKLAHOMA, UNITED STATES OF AMERICA

Norman, Oklahoma

2012

MONGREL EMPIRE PRESS
NORMAN, OK

ONLINE CATALOGUE: WWW.MONGRELEMPIRE.ORG

This publisher is a proud member of

$$\left[\, \mathbf{clmp} \,\right]$$

COUNCIL OF LITERARY MAGAZINES & PRESSES
W W W . C L M P . O R G

Book Design: Mongrel Empire Press using iWork Pages.

In remembrance of SFC Randy Rhen,
SGT Todd Robbins,
&
SPC Donald Oaks

So it goes—Kurt Vonnegut

ACKNOWLEDGEMENTS

The author gratefully acknowledges the editors of the following publications, in which versions of the poems first appeared:

"Medivac" and "Convoy" in *Gold Mine*
"High Stakes" and "Damned Kids" in *New Mexico Poetry Review*
"Dear Mr. Sandman" and *Mind at War*, artwork, in *Connecticut Review*
"Red Fields," "Baghdad International," "Fort Sill's New Housing Division" and "Nanna's
Blackberry Cobbler" in *Sugar Mule* and reprinted in *Ain't Nobody That Can Sing Like Me*

Versions of the following poems were published in a collection titled *In the Rubble at Our Feet*, a chapbook published by Rose Rock Press in 2011:

"Desert Hostel"
"High Stakes"
"Slack-Twisted Fellow"
"Hydrating Flies"
"Who dat is?"
"Baghdad International"
"The Last Time We Talked"
"ATACMS in the Night"
"In the Rubble at Our Feet"
"I am the Blood"
"Blackhawk Medevac"
"We Called Him Martha Stewart"
"Never Night"
"Hero"
"Welcome Home"
"Where the Veterans Are"
"From One Veteran to Another"
"What Makes the Green Grass Grow"

CONTENTS

FOREWORD

I had heard about Jason from colleagues before I met him: an Iraq War veteran who wanted very much to be a writer. That he took two of my classes was my good fortune as a teacher because Jason not only fills a desk, but also considerably improves the atmosphere in any room in which he sits.

A genuine student as distinguished, in the terms of one of my early college professors, from mere enrollees, Jason has worked hard and willingly accepted instruction and guidance as he has learned and grown. Other students have enjoyed success in my composition and literature classes, to be sure, but I have seldom enjoyed the presence of students who learned things and applied what they learned as quickly as Jason did. As opposed to other students in creative writing classes who are generally young and have a Romantic notion of what it means to be a writer (especially true of aspiring poets), but who discover rather quickly that they have had little real experience and thus have little to say (a category into which in retrospect I as a college student certainly fit), Jason has had important things to say and demons to exorcise from the beginning. Not just motivated, then, but burning to learn, he has actively claimed an education in Adrienne Rich's terms.

My first class experience with Jason still stands out. In Techniques of Poetry, a form-and-theory course in poetry that also features a workshop component, he quickly distinguished himself as the best student. The other students recognized that he was the best, but were not envious, by the way, because of his abundant kindness, generosity, and positive outlook. To those outside of that classroom, recognition of his growing ability came quickly. A poem he workshopped that semester, "High Stakes," a revised version of which appears in this collection, was the next semester chosen by an independent judge as the first-prize winner in a poetry contest for which I put up the money at my university. In my mind, what makes Jason's success all the more remarkable is that he had not been especially bookish prior to his war experience and in fact was first required to complete a remedial composition class because of a low test score.

Jason was indeed a novice poet when he took that class, but in the relatively short time since, he has grown into a poet of no small achievement because he has never stopped reading, writing, thinking, and applying what he learns. He has made analogous effort beyond his writing, too, finishing in short order a BA in English, embarking upon and completing an MA in Education, and then becoming a high school English teacher valued by students, colleagues, and administrators alike.

Though he was once technically my student, Jason has from the beginning been teaching me about the Iraq War, and he will soon instruct you, too. Welcome to that world, and his.

John Morris
Cameron University

I. POST-THEATER

RED FIELDS

*I remembered Sulayma when the passion
of battle was as fierce
as the passion of my body when we parted.*

*I thought I saw, among the lances, the tall
perfection of her body,
and when they bent toward me I embraced them.*

—Abu-L-Hasan IBN Al-Qabturnuh, "In Battle"
translated from Arabic by Lysander Kemp

My feet sink
into the Barnestilled soil
of my father-in-law's
Oklahoma land,
reminding me of times
before I met his daughter,
when I drove along
in a tank convoy
towards Baghdad
at the same
pace as a tractor
over an unplowed field.

With each stop,
we would have fifteen minutes
to dig two foxholes,
with e-tools
better designed for
digging 1'x1' cat-holes.

When the sand was soft
like the overworked
edges of the short-rows
of my father-in-law's fields,
it was a blessing.
We'd dig our holes deep,
safe, to plant ourselves into
if we came under fire,
so we could rise out
when the lead rain ended.

When the sand was as hard
as the unworked
ground hiding under
the buffalo grass,
our e-tools would chink
at the surface with every hit;
our holes would be shallow,
and we'd push the sand up around
the perimeter, making
a false reservoir of safety,
knowing bullets would penetrate
the powdered walls if we were ambushed,
and our bodies would lie
half-exposed in shallow graves,
in pools coloring the sand
Oklahoma clay.

When his daughter was only
a pin-up girl in my mind,
the sandstorms would erase
the foxholes after we pushed forward;
now I drive my father-in-law's tractor
and set the plow into the soil
to cultivate his land.

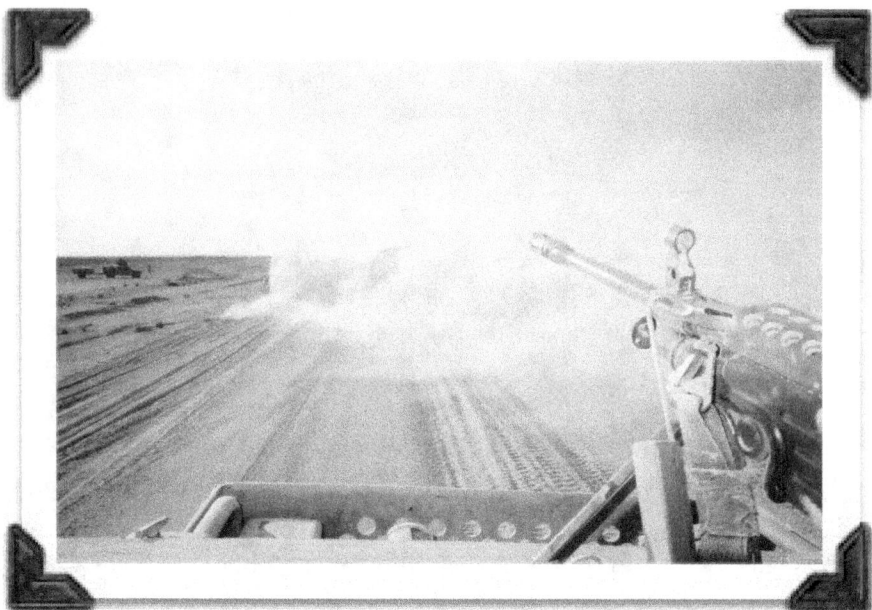

DEAR MR. SANDMAN

I probably killed you—
But there is no way of knowing
I flipped the switch two days ago,

and you haven't been in that ditch long,
just since you crawled there for safety
like a cockroach sprayed with Raid,
never dying on contact but just after,
or maybe, when the first unit passed,
they treated you like road-kill
and placed you to the side.

The flies that swarm you
feast on me too;
but at least you don't have to worry
about the Baghdad Boils and dysentery—
I was up itching and shitting all last night.

Thank you for being
content with your burial.
—No casket, your charred limbs sprawl out;
a few thin sheets of sand
make your face unrecognizable
and congeal your wounds,
but are unable to conceal
the burned-blackness of your skin.

I will not be able to attend your ceremony,
except to place your body into a bag.
—Then I'll hold you briefly in my arms
and know you forever,
see you lurking in the crowds
at the grocery store or the mall;
you'll follow me
into the liquor store,
and keep me company
when I'm at home alone,
and we'll each have a drink.

POST-GRATIFICATION DISORDER

My handprint reddens on her bare breast. I
awake to see her clutch her chest. My whole
head aching, I see no desert sand — my
M-16 missing from my side. I stole
her breath as she awoke and winced in pain.
I dare a glance into her enraged glare,
and her midnight lips ask, "Are you insane?"
She becomes my buddy with his blank stare.
"What are you looking at? I have to go."
Now I see her again. "Please no, don't leave."
Shoving on her high heels she says, "I know
your type," then shoots an arm through a coat sleeve:
    The door slams, and artillery fires — I
    hit the floor, shiver there naked, and cry.

FROM ONE VETERAN TO ANOTHER

"It's okay to sleep with the lights on,"
he tells me as I watch him caress his beer
bottle with ringless fingers;
    he's been married twice,
two children with the first.

I ask him how old his kids are.
His fingers climb
to the middle of the bottle
and erect his cigarette like a flagpole
    without a flag
atop the Corona that he tilts
     to his lips.

I watch the white foam slosh
back down into the yellow glass.
He looks at my clean-shaven face,
takes a long drag.

"The youngest is about your age," he replies
—the thick air of his exhale clouds my head.
Politely,
I stand fast at his side.
"You can call me anytime
you need to talk," he says. "4:00 a.m.,
that's okay, I'll be awake anyway."

I tell him thanks and I will,
    though I'll lose his number
at the next bar or strip club,
or leave it in my pocket
when I wash my smoky,
perfumed jeans the following day.

DAMNED KIDS

Outside of Walter Reed,
the cloth-patched holes in my legs burn with each step I take
as I attempt to lift myself from a wheelchair
and walk for the first time since I returned home;
while I stare down at the Velcro shoes I was given at Landstuhl,
laughter invades my ears.

I lift my head and see kids playing soccer
in the shadows of the D.C. monuments,
wearing Nikes, Reeboks, and sponsored jerseys,
on manicured greens with articulate white lines,
fields that appear artificial except for the smell
of the freshly cut grass that sticks to my shoes.

The opposing teams battle to kick balls into radiant orange nets,
and their laugher is almost the same as the Iraqi children
who kicked around my empty water bottle,
some shoeless, some shirtless, without teams, rules, time, or
points,
under a dry, relentless sun, over unmarked sand fields.
The pain, searing now, collapses me back into my chair.

A ref blows his whistle at half, and the kids run for the sidelines,
converging to gather oranges, bananas, and Gatorades from iced
coolers
supplied by parents who smile at their children as they devour
their snacks.

A scud siren howls, and the skinny, sun-darkened Iraqi children
run to a cement bunker; they crumble and share the poppy seed
pound cake
from my MRE as I clean my M-16.

When the "all clear" is given,
the children return to their fields,
and I return to Walter Reed.

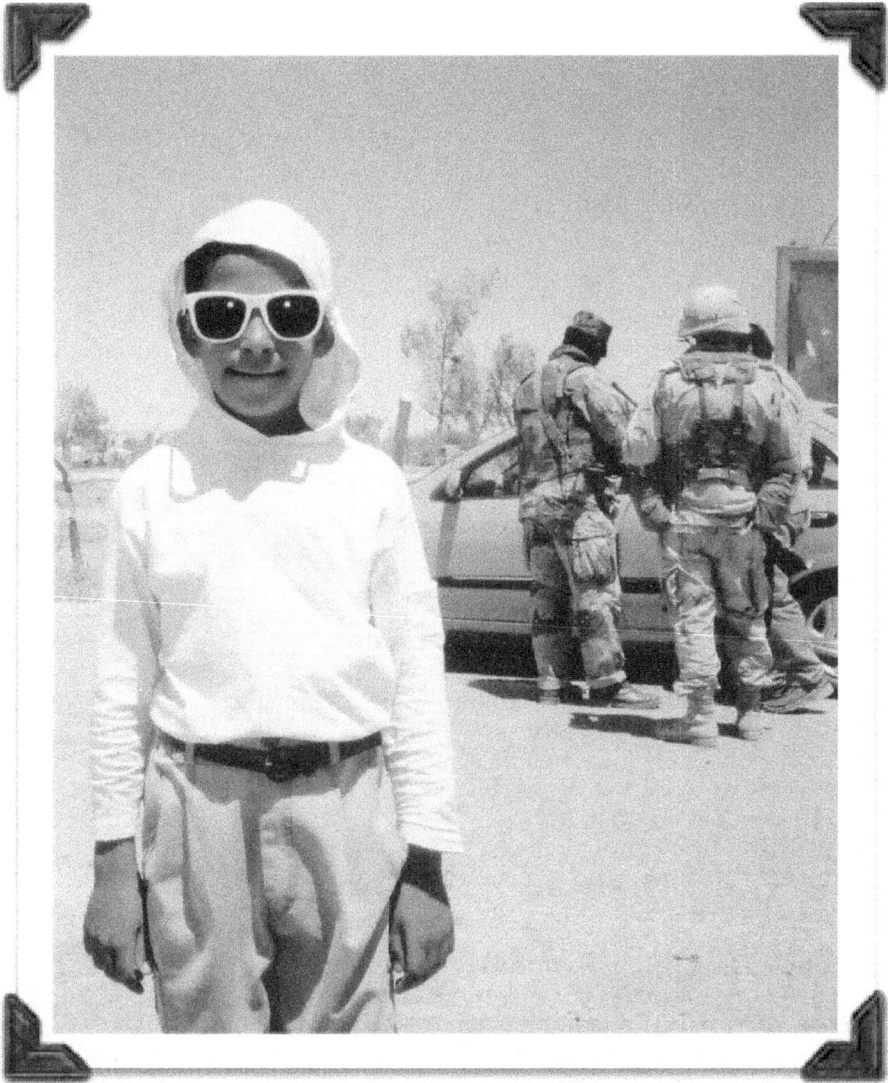

Subjects of Merriment

*I was pretty well through with the subject. At one time or
another I had probably considered it from most of its
various angles, including the one that certain injuries or
imperfections are a subject of merriment while remaining
quite serious for the person possessing them . . .
Undressing, I looked at myself in the mirror . . . I suppose
it was funny.*

—Hemingway, *The Sun Also Rises*

"So you were wounded?"
"Yeah."

He scans my body with bold eyes,
taking inventory of every limb,
wondering if he miscounted
when he first saw me,
and almost as if without control,
his widening pupils
move southward,
pulling his whole head down
until his gaze is upon my pant-legs.

I want to tell him the right one's gone,
watch those eyes expand
waiting for me to lift the shroud,
as if the sight of a titanium rod
would somehow allow him to experience the war
and connect us like brothers
so he could tell the stories of war
tomorrow at work.

But I think of LT, now legless,
and how unfunny, and unfriendly,
friendly fire is.

"No, you can't see my wounds," I tell him,
considering making reference to Jake Barnes.
Not wanting him to get the wrong impression,
I tell him Forrest Gump.
And he asks, "So you got shot in the ass?" with a smirk.
I explain that it was shrapnel,
entered the side and went out the back.

"Exit only," I tell him. He laughs,
and I recall watching LT on TV
sprinting down a field on two rods
that matched the one he gripped in his hands
as he played lacrosse in the traditional scrimmage match
between the Army and Navy alumni teams
–he was captain when he was at West Point.

During the post-game interview,
the camera panned out to capture
LT's full figure as he responded
to the reporter's question
about the Army Alumni's recent loss.
"I've never been too quick
on my feet anyway," he replied,
and for a moment, I laugh a little too.

BLACK ANGUS WATERMELON

"2010 Rush Springs Watermelon Festival overall winner:
Black Diamond, 149 pounds"

The flies cover the bodies
on the Iraqi fields like
the backs of black angus,
but their muscles never jerk,
already swollen too tight
within their skin.

I feel the flies on my skin
and swish my hand
like a heifer swishes its tail,
waving the flies off
but there is no reprieve;

I want his hand
to do the same,
but it's as still
as the rest of him.

I reach down and touch him,
feel the flies embedding,
crawling around beneath my skin
just under the surface, just like his,
just like the black seeds
in the half-split watermelon
I watch my niece eat
standing on the porch,

the red stickiness
covering her naked body
from grinning lips to
tapping toes, dripping
onto the shadowed
concrete beneath
her feet.

A CORPSE WALKED INTO THE BUS STATION TODAY

His arms swung his clenched fists
with purpose as he marched in,
stomping his left, dragging his right,
surrounded by ash.
He hadn't been dead long;
his DCUs still smelled of sand
and smoke,
his buzzed hair, singed –still smoldered
and he only had a limp.

He placed his fists on the counter
on the opposite side of the ticket window
and met my stare.

'I need a one-way back to Iraq,' he said.

I leaned toward the hole in the
glass between us. "I'm sorry, sir-"

-'I'm no officer, I work for a living!'
He cut me off with a voice as gruff as he looked.

I leaned back, "Sorry, Sergeant-"

'-Are you calling me a sorry Sergeant?'
He said with a voice
that rattled my notepad
of lost bags off the counter,

but I didn't flinch.

"No Sergeant, and I'm sorry, but
no corpses are allowed on the bus."

He slammed his fists
on the counter and
one finger fell off
to the floor.
'Say again?'

I could feel the heat of his breath
through the hole in the glass,
but I had been trained on
how to handle hostile customers;

I pulled out the Greyhound Bus Manual
and slid it half through the ticket slot –

"R-right here Sergeant."
I put my finger on corpses,
right between
compressed gasses
and cremated remains.

His face tightened:
'You tellin' me my driver can't go back either?'

He looked back
at the pile of ash
that had settled slightly
behind him to the left.

"Sergeant, I'm sorry."

His fists shattered the glass
down onto the book.

He put his good hand
around my neck;

my skin crawled with flames;
my blood turned to napalm.
As my vision dwindled,
I focused on the manual.

"Sergeant," I said.

His grip eased and
through a jagged piece of glass
I read,

"The policy only covers
checked bags."

He released.
I caught my breath:

"But I have no buses
to Iraq, only home."

14

Nanna's Blackberry Cobbler

The smell, bitter and biting
at my taste buds, ignites
saliva and concaves my cheeks.

The crust crumbles
as my fork slices
into the blackberries
that bleed onto my plate;

I see and feel the warmth
as I bring the first forkful forward,
tasting it before the cobbler reaches my lips.

I sit in Papa's rocking chair
on the cracked cement porch,
slow creaks crescendoing
and decrescendoing from the rockers
—while I run
to my artillery unit's perimeter,
weapon in hand.

I stare out with dilated,
unblinking eyes
over a glowing, flat terracotta horizon,
filled with the silhouettes of angus cattle
casting moving shadows that stretch
from the fields to the porch.
 —locked with fear,
my heart pulsing in my clenched fists
is my only movement;
over the shaking muzzle of an M-16,
I watch as my shadow advances
outside the perimeter
into the live dunes.

A dust devil dies to the north
after passing across Papa's dry summer fields;
cobbler continues bleeding on my plate;
my feet hasten their heel-to-toe roll;
—I quiver, facing out into a night
tunneled by the fire behind me,
but I cannot look back; I'm on guard,
and the medevac has been called.

The shouts and screams
—all men—emerging
from the flames of a Humvee
echo within my head, until they are muffled
by the whomping blades of a Blackhawk
that stir sand and smoke around
me, and I disappear like
an egg yolk into a country-
cobbler batter.

FORT SILL'S NEW HOUSING DIVISION

*Military bases name buildings, roads, training areas, and
everything else after highly decorated soldiers, retired
soldiers, soldiers killed in action, or people the military
killed or captured. Geronimo's grave and Geronimo Road
can also be found on Fort Sill.*

I find Roberts Road.

    His freckles sink down,
        the color of his lips runs off
            into his white, opaque skin
                that sags down
                    like a sheet
                        placed over his face.
            Subtle red and blue lines,
                like broken glass
                    that stays intact,
                        show through.
                            A dark worm of red stretches out
                            from his lips down
                                to the gurney at his back.

I see him finishing
    right after me around the track,
    his gray PT shirt clinging to his heaving chest,
    his freckles shimmering under sweat.
    His crimson lips form a smile.
    I smile back and nod,
    knowing he didn't make time
    for max points,
    but with no heart
    to tell him he didn't.
    He trains me on push-ups
    and sit-ups during the week;
    on the weekend,
    if his wife permits,
    I train him on the run.

I turn left onto Williams Road.

    He stands guard half out of the top
        of an armored Humvee.
            A bomb hits and he is almost severed
                at the waist. The medics cut
                    off his blood-saturated DCUs,
                        set his intestines in place,
                            and bandage his other wounds.
            But the bleeding doesn't stop.
                He makes it onto the Blackhawk
                but never gets off.

I see him in my peripheral
   standing at attention.
   I curse his creased,
   dark green BDUs
   that make my month-old
   set look wrinkled and faded,
   his Kiwi boots that outshine mine,
   which I spent hours on
   the night before.
   The platoon sergeant praises him
   and then steps over to me.
   After cursing Williams, I ask him,
   and he shares his military secrets with me,
   like he shared his life secrets
   with his fiancé.

I turn right onto Rogers Road.

    He can't be found at first.
        He took the impact of the bomb.
            They piece him back together,
                no gauze or tape necessary,
            lace all that can be found
                of him into one bag with
                    his dog tags for identification
                and send him home
                    to his wife and daughters.

I see him in his dress blues
    at the Saint Barbara's Ball;
    I admire his many rows of ribbons,
    his tight high-and-tight,
    the shine of the brass U.S. and cross cannons
    on his lapel. He is the complete package
    of military bearing, the NCO on the
    Army commercials.
    I watch him smile
    toward his wife
    and her return.
    I don't approach him
  with the smudge on my brass U.S.

I keep searching for my road.

    Shrapnel pierces my back,
        weaving through organs and bones,
            only serrating muscle,
                leaving me perforated, but intact.
    My blood strains out of my body,
            but with several field bandages
                my blood coagulates.
                    My lungs keep filling with air.

My PT shirt clings to my chest
    after I pump out the max
    pushups and sit-ups
    while I await the run.

    I press my BDUs with an iron
    and can of spray starch an extra time
    just before formation.
    After heating my kiwi with a lighter,
    I poor it lightly over
    the toes of my boots,
    then begin to shine.

    I remove the smudge
    off my brass
    and call my girlfriend
    to apologize
    for the fight
    we had the night before.

Welcome Home

His face
    is upon a placard
thrust upward by his mother;

I almost don't recognize him
    without a smile
    with his California skin,
Marine cap and American flag
    at his back.

I see his face from the backseat
    of a convertible driven by
    a Vietnam veteran, and
I smile and hand out salutes like candy
    to every flag we pass as
April flakes of snow descend
    in dense clumps on the
    first Klamath Falls

"Support our Soldiers" parade.

    When the parade ends,
Bryan's mom approaches me
    in Veteran's Park.

With her placard still clenched in one hand,
    she wraps her arms around me
    as if I were her son.
Smile gone, I embrace her,
    but I don't know where
    to put my hands, my arms,
    which way to tilt my head.
I am awkward,
    so I hold her
    until she is done.

20

WHERE THE VETERANS ARE

She serves your food
At your favorite restaurant
Because she couldn't
Concentrate on college,
So her GI Bill stopped paying.

He mows your lawn
Because he has trouble with authority,
Especially the high-school-aged
Assistant-manager type
Like the ones at the restaurants.

They work as janitors
Because they have no problem
Cleaning urinals, especially
During the night shift
When no one else is around,
And they don't mind
When a job well done
Goes unnoticed.

He cries during commercials
Because he was shot, and
He knows a buddy
Without legs,
And he watched another die
Beside him.

She is homeless,
Attempting to reconnect
With her basic needs,
Those they lost,
And the time
They all really lived.

He's digging a foxhole
To lie down into
Beside his buddies
Because he's tired
Of his life after death.

POST-THEATER

When I close my eyes, the movie projector clicks on; a burning Humvee is on the screen. The soda machine starts dispensing an adrenaline drip as I listen to the popcorn pop of rounds cooking off until a smell more potent than burnt popcorn fills the theater. In my lap I feel dampness; looking down I see blood: shrapnel shot from the screen through my thighs. I get up to leave and realize I can't walk; the movie keeps reeling, and the images of my buddies' dead bodies illuminate the theater. I low-crawl up stairs, slipping in a waterfall of adrenaline, to find the projector room locked. "Turn it off, turn it off!" I yell. My voice startles me; I raise the screen, and immediately I am immersed into the scene, surrounded by sand that sticks to my cold, sweating body.

SOMETIMES

I want to burrow
deep beneath into
your safe, peaceful place
—lid shut down tight,
warm under frozen
Michigan soil,
and become you
with your wax-filled,
shrapnel-torn
     holes,
so you will not be lonely
and will have no thought
of how easily
you could have been me:
your holes
would have slowly filled
with flesh, and you could
have returned to duty until
retirement—like you planned—
and you wouldn't
have to worry about
how helpless you
looked, staring
up at me unable to move,
and your mother
could have celebrated
instead of cried
at your arrival.

Your Voice

At home in our closet,
on a message machine,
on a little black tape,
I keep your voice
from the last time
I missed your call.

You tell me,
"I'll be home soon, I love you, I miss you,"
'til the beep cuts off your lies.
But I play it again and again,
your voice keeping me company
as I light up my first Marlboro in five years

and drink my Coors Light
until I can believe you,
drink more
until we are sitting on the porch
drunk together,
the heat of your breath
against my cheek
as you slur a whisper into my ear
about how you will make love to me tonight,
but I just laugh, knowing

your hands will start riding up my shirt,
I'll fail to undo your buckle,
you'll spill beer on the carpet,
but I won't care,
and we'll lie on the couch
half-undressed, limbs entangled
until the heat is too much,
and I'll wake up sweating
with a pounding head
in the middle of the night
and stagger down the narrow hall
of our one-bedroom apartment
to our California king.

TAINTED

1.

My tainted toenails
with browning cuticles crumble
under clippers, brittle from
three years ago, from a year
confined in sweat-saturated black socks,
locked in black leather
boots with weathered laces.

The military doctor
prescribed some pills and generic Lamasil,
but I've had enough rashes
and diarrhea, and the convoy
stopped for no one,
but I'm not embarrassed
—I wasn't the only one; one tanker
shit himself three times.

Fatigue,
that side-effect I can handle,
so I swallow a pill
and lie down to sleep;
I fold the covers under and around
my crusty feet, creating a pocket
my wife calls my cocoon
—she's not allowed in.

2.

I see my feet clean;
then I realize
they're my father's from
a time when he had
dark, short hair and
a tight, trimmed mustache,
and I am pulling off his boots and socks
as he sits in the recliner
in front of the TV after duty;
his feet are unlike mine, but
it's not his fault; he volunteered
for Vietnam and got sent to Alaska
because the conflict was
coming to an end.

3.

My wife walks on the
balls of her feet into the bedroom
and climbs in bed beside me
—My body jerks me awake with
a force that shakes both sides of the bed.

I listen to our dog bark, watch
lights move across the room
as cars drive by.

I watch over her as she sleeps,
not because I love her, which I do,
but because I am on guard:
my body tense,
my eyes won't close.

4.

Then I feel the scathing
wind across my face,
the burn of sand in my eyes.
I'm walking,
boots slipping
with every step in loose sand;
my bones drive my body forward
as my calves and thighs feel
more like swollen water bags
than muscles;
I feel the collar of my flack vest,
damp and dirty, brushing
against my neck,
my chest constricted
and my body
weighted down
by my combat loaded LBE,
and Kevlar—with bracket
and NVGs
attached.

5.

I hear no blast,
but I am on my back,
deaf, watching flames,
watching a soldier
running with a
fire extinguisher
—I can't move.

6.

"Huh-huh-huh,"
is all I can mutter
as I try to say, "Wake up, damn it."
"Wake me, damn it."
 But I can't wake up,

and I know why she hesitates—
I jump no matter how she wakes me,
and we don't talk about last time.
Fuck, I jump all the time:
when I run into her in the hall,
when she makes a noise in the kitchen,
or puts the dog out,
but we don't talk about that either.
—Now I'm awake, panting,
and she's awake, standing
at the edge of the bed, ready
to run or crawl back into bed.

7.

We haven't slept together
in more than a month;
it's been even longer
since we've had sex.

I sleep with my hand on my
.45, under my pillow.
She pleaded
with tear-filled eyes to put
the gun away; she
told me she won't
sleep another night with me
until I do.

She's sleeping in bed
tonight as I sleep
on the couch with
my hand on my .45,
sleeping better
without her.

8.

I call my dad and tell
him I don't think she loves me
anymore, and he tells me
I should let her wash my feet.
—I fake a forced laugh—
as if he made a joke.
He tells me about Jesus,
about how he washed the
feet of his disciples. Then he
says, "Maybe after you talk to her,
you could let Jesus wash your feet."
—I hang up the phone.

9.

My wife and I sit, together,
on the couch before bed.
I tell her about my battle buddy's dead body
beside me, and his face
fills our five-by-five living room
—mouth open, eyes closed
as if trying to catch snowflakes
but his tongue's stuck
at the back of his throat.

We sit on the couch together
within his head,
looking at each other
through the fog
of his cold skin.

II. WHILE WE WERE WAITING

DESERT HOSTEL

Our skin turns
the grey of the dead,
rippling like flesh submerged
in liquid too long,
and the creases
in the valleys of our hands
turn to creeks,

but we will not feel the satisfaction
of water over our bodies
until we are done.

Heat piles into waves
atop the horizons
and tan currents scrape
away our hydration like
Roman slaves with strigils,
invading our every orifice,
asphyxiating our pores.

The sun-baked sand scorches
through the soles
of our suffocating combat boots,
souring our socks,
yellowing and softening the nails of our toes,
decomposing the skin of our feet.

Dried out,
our flesh falls off in clumps;
our muscles shrivel
like sucked-dry Camelbaks,
and we stand in formation
naked, until our exposed tendons dry
into strips of jerky;

our carcasses fall clanking
into one copious pile,
and the desert dogs
howl and sneer at one another
as they gnaw on our bones,
swallowing our marrow.

HIGH STAKES

One of four soldiers who sleep
in this three-man tent
is always on guard duty,
and around this empty holdem-cot,
rank doesn't matter.

A red chem-light, won by barter
from the supply specialist, glows,
turning even the hearts and diamonds black
as it dangles from a five-fifty cord noose
tied to the lumber two-by-four tent pole;

the pot fills with soldiers' antes:
a can of peanuts, two cigarettes,
a half can of Skoal –buy in
with a twenty-dollar bill
and question their decision
to let you play
because the peanuts were from
a mother, the cigarettes a brother,
the Skoal a friend back home.

When the pot contains
a full pack of cigarettes
and a sealed bag of Red Man leaf cut,
the buy-in easily doubles to forty,
but out of boredom you pay
to gamble with something other than your life
for a change,
to win a pack of smokes
you can relax with,
or a sealed bag of dip
that can be used to celebrate
or just ante up another game.

WHAT'S FOR DINNER, DOC?

Inside my Coke-can-armored Humvee,
I swelter in my flack vest,
feeling like Bugs Bunny, boiling
in a bathtub-sized pot,
singing along with the dancing little Indian
who is preparing him for dinner.

The solemn Iraqi children
stare at me with
starving big, black eyes
with sleepless, deep, brown bags
on a dried-up palette,
which is accompanied
by their dance,
a synchronized, sombering
movement of the hand
tapping the tip of the tongue.

I tear off the corner
of a bag of Skittles from my MRE
and toss it so it spins
and sprinkles Skittles from the sky
like on the commercials
back home they know nothing about;
they scurry around
collecting the colorful candies,
then scamper off,
leaving subtle dimples
in the sand.

I ask my BC
where their parents are;
he tells me
they're awaiting us
behind the dunes,
and I wonder if
I made the right
turn in Albuquerque.

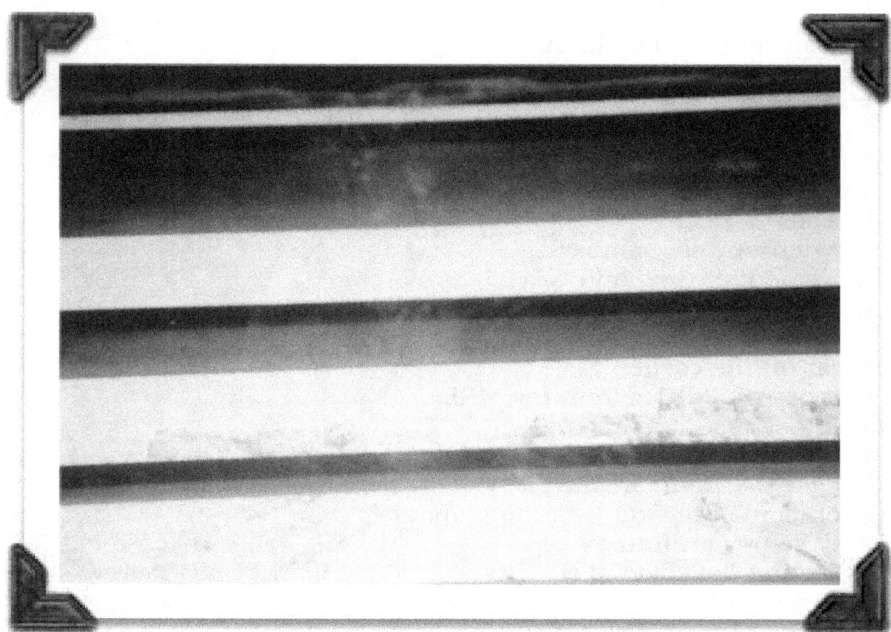

I HEARD A FLY BUZZ

I stare out
A sand-fogged windshield
The size of a postcard
At a scene that
Could be drawn
With one horizontal line.

A fly loops
Around the
Enclosed cab,
Buzzing; he lands
On my face.

Swat—miss.

He flies before
My eyes, mocking,
Moving freely
As I sit cramped.

He lands
On my ears,
Chin,
Lips.

I slowly open
My mouth.

His legs tickle
As he walks in.

—I close.

My first kill.

WHILE WE WERE WAITING: MARCH '03

The tent wars started while we waited on the border
in tents with sand floors, still on training orders,
with live 5.56 rounds, grenades, and rockets.

After returning from the mess truck and eating our T-rat dinner,
complemented with a slice of bread and a packet of jelly,
we found the inside of our tent looking like a glowing Pollock
painting; the contents of a green chem-light spotted our cots
and sleeping bags and clung in patches all the way up
to the cathedral peak of our tent liner.

In retaliation, each of us who slept in the tent
saved up the heaters and Tabasco from our MRE lunches
for the next week, and we created our own chemical arsenal.

The soldier from our tent with the midnight guard shift
invaded the neighboring tent and added water
to the bottle containing the concoction,
releasing a geyser of nontoxic, nonetheless extremely potent, gas,
and as we were trained in basic when ambushing a bunker,
he opened their tent flap, dropped in the improvised device,
closed the door, and took cover.

One soldier scrambled out in boxers and boots—gas mask on,
another just wearing DCU bottoms, the next in full chemical gear.
The next day, the tent next door from the one we hit
owned up to the chem-light raid.

That night, the president gave his speech.
It wasn't during my shift so I was asleep, resting up
for tomorrow's strike.

SLACK-TWISTED FELLOW

> . . . he had good strength to work at times; but the times
> could not be relied on to coincide with the hours of
> requirement; and, having been unaccustomed to the
> regular toil of the day-labourer, he was not particularly
> persistent when they did so coincide.
> —Thomas Hardy, *Tess of the d'Urbervilles*

We just called 'em shitbags in the Army;
Pvt. Phillips was one, placed on extra-duty for pissin' hot.
He never really did much when on duty,
so to him it was really just duty.

He was still on extra-duty when we deployed,
and when in Iraq, his punishment was extended
when he was caught with contraband, *Penthouse*,
though we don't think it was ever discarded after confiscation.

He was placing sandbags atop a reinforced plywood roof
covering a three-man bunker he had been diggin'
the past three days when the colonel walked by.

"Dig that yourself private?" he asked with a grin.
"Sir, yes sir."
The colonel looked around and saw nothing
but closed-up, sand-colored tents.

"We need more soldiers like you in today's Army,"
the colonel said, flipping him a coin;
Pvt. Philips caught it in the air.
"Sir, yes sir."

FRED

I wonder what he thought
when he awoke surrounded
by a unit of troops, if he hissed in his
hole while the ground rattled
and his cave collapsed
as we set up camp.

There was nothing
there except him, and
after we left, nothing.
A night maneuver claimed his life,
a friendly drive-over incident.

We held a lower-enlisted
funeral for him, complete with
weapon in the ground with boots
and helmet labeled "Fred,"
our first casualty, our first kill.

DESERT COLLIE

I conduct my hourly march
around the caravan,
hear their human-laughing howls,
crave to shoot,
but have no line-of-sight.

I see one in the daylight,
nose to ground, surviving,
black-and-white furry bones,
not a dingo, or coyote,
but Border Collie mix.

Squinting,
I see there's another roaming with it,
Jack-Russell, runt-of-a-dog;
I look for the white picket fence
they broke from behind,
but the scenery hasn't changed.

I watch: myself throw a ball,
they fight over it,
until one returns it;
I teach them tricks,
give them treats,
scratch their heads,
rub their bellies,

until my vehicle slams down over a dune;
the cab jolts up and down,
a rough, growling idle
whines inside the cab
and I bounce off the seat
as my driver yells, "Hang on!"

The metallic pings and pops
of the flexing metal of our chassis
combined with the moans and groans
of our shifting load
remind me of my duty.

The dogs flee from our encroaching vehicles
just like the coyotes and camels,
and the clouds of exhaust
and sand from our convoy
engulf them,
but I have already forgotten.

DESERT ROSE

The bottles we drank from,
we refilled from the cut-out bottoms,
their tops taped to hollow tent poles
erected in the sand,

clusters of them
with accommodating heights
staggered around the outskirts of camp
like flower arrangements.
Makeshift stalls surrounded
the arrangements to our east
—the unit over there contained females.

When we left,
we left nothing behind,
not even our flower arrangements
or Old Chuck,
who we all had become fond of,
our wooden stall made just for shitting.

We burned what we couldn't take:
tarps, tables, trash all blackened,
heating up the air,
making the sand think
it was day again
as we followed our shadows
back to our vehicles.

From then on,
after use, the quart-sized bottles
were left intact
and used on the go.
filled, sealed, and tossed
out the window,
for there was no stopping
until we finished
once we began to move.

HYDRATING FLIES

When you drown a fly,
It will appear dead
Until you tap salt on it,
And it comes back to life
Like a magician whose
Life is the real trick.

The flies come to life
In swarms from the sand;
They knew we would be back
And just waited, and as soon as our
Tracks disturbed them,
Awoke to quench
Their thirst.

WHO DAT IS?

We pass on roving guard,
0100, 0200, 0300;
his shadow approaches
mine, and tonight

I've run out
of creative ways
to use "pumpkin"
in a sentence,
and to be honest,

I don't even know
if that is still the challenge,
and I don't care to learn
the new one,
if there is one,

because no one else will
know it, or the password
either. So I simply ask
"Who dat is?"

and the shadow responds
with the same question,
in a voice I recognize, so
I know not to blow
his fucking head off.

CONVOY

One hundred and ten miles is a short distance
to the beach on a pleasant summer day.

At ten miles per hour, on a beach with no ocean,
immersed in a sandstorm that limits your line-of-sight
to that of a tank picked up by a small child
and thrust front-first into the sand,
you won't be arriving 'til after dark.

You move while nearly blind during the day
and brake hard often, during each brief interlude,
that you see -a foot away- the sand-colored,
covered tank stopped in front of you.

After missing the sunset on the ocean,
darkness falls and you become entranced
by the two red dots you must follow,
dancing like a pair of flirting fireflies
across your windshield.

When the black-out drive lights vanish, you stop;
the tank in front of you made a sudden ninety-degree turn
or dropped off a sandy cliff;
if it was hit by mortar fire or an IED, you'd know.
You see the red dots through a side window,
and you re-align.

After pivoting, you resume driving,
Dreaming that when you arrive at your final destination
it will be at the ocean, to play with the child
with the little green army tank on the beach,
and you can remove it from its sandy grave,
teach him about an armistice,
and turn his toy towards the sunset.

SMOKER'S PATCH

This smoker's patch is not for
quitting but staying alive.

It's the burned-out patch of fabric
on the inner thigh
of a desert smoker's DCUs.

It's a crude,
callused patch of skin
from a rude,
necessary wakening
by the singe of a cigarette
dropped from a sleeping soldier's hand
onto his own inner thigh.

18 AND PREPARED TO DIE

Now I lay me
down to sleep
if I die before
I wake

I will be able
to breathe
I will return home
sooner than expected

My niece and nephew
will go to college

they'll remember me
Amen.

III: WELCOME TO IRAQ

WELCOME TO IRAQ

With a blue background and
white reflective writing,
the sign shines against the
blank night,
squiggly lines
translated into
English underneath;
it says,

"Welcome to Iraq"

just as if it were saying,

"Welcome to California,"

and I snap a shot
for a souvenir
on a digital camera
the sand will soon ruin.

BAGHDAD INTERNATIONAL

The ninety-four left of 3-13 Field Artillery, Red Dragon Battalion,
drove over bumps by night, bodies by day;
then in the afternoons, they bagged
the scrunched, scorched remains from yesterday's artillery fires,
to clear their claim of the Baghdad airport.

Then they guarded their plot
with .50 cals, M-249s, 16s, and 203s,
weapons unable to distinguish between civilians
and suicide bombers,
and futile against the harpy-sized, flesh-eating flies
that would invade night and day, every day.

Nineteen miles and two days south of Baghdad,
four Dragons went to Heaven, at least we presume;
their Bibles were recovered.
They traveled by means of burning in a Humvee
lit up by an Air Force bomb.

Three others were medevacted out,
detached from the ninety-four
as our limbs were detached from our bodies,
saved from witnessing the airport
by means of shrapnel, bullets, and a Blackhawk;
we flew south as the unit continued on the road home.

The soldier's legs on the stretcher beside me
had apparently sinned or traveled upward prematurely
because they didn't accompany us any longer,
nor did what looks my other buddy had;
his face now looks as if it were rained on
by burning shrapnel, which it was.

The ninety-four rose from Baghdad by means of a 747.
They returned to what once was home.
At least the only other man to go through Hell and arise
went straight to Heaven after.

They entered another damnation
full of divorce decrees, drugs, and broken bank accounts;
some brought the death back with them,
just as we all brought back our badge,
and their families got to go through it too.

Few returned to a moment's awkward embrace
of a family knowingly never understanding.
But each of the ninety-four still had each other
until car accidents, drug overdoses, and return deployments
began to pick them off like a sniper, one by one.

RED-BROWN DAYS

Under and through howling winds,
we push
during the pulsing, red-brown days
—following glimpses
of the vehicle before us,
—following the Plugger's waypoints
at an almost stagnant
pace: NW, NE, North.

When red-brown darkens
to brown-black,
through NVGs, the night
pulses green with IEDS,
mortars, and small arms fire;

one line, we continue,
like serpentine vertebrae
stalking, heat-seeking,
closer, closer
to Baghdad.

THE LAST TIME WE TALKED

He had much to say;
my stretcher was
slid-up beside his.
I didn't hold
him in my arms.
I was bleeding;
he had bled.
I didn't know.

"Sgt Rob!"

He didn't answer.
We traveled to-
gether in the back
of a deuce-and-
a-half, for a mile
and a half, to
a medevac point.

ATACMS IN THE NIGHT

Launched with the force
Of Orion's eternally drawn-back bow,
The rockets sail through the night sky,
Forming a constellation of shooting stars,
Tactical missiles that launch in silence
Except for their sonic boom.
The missiles launched
From up to 100 kilometers away;
We never see houses, intact,
Or faces, alive.

ARTILLERY KILL

I flipped a switch:
The rocket launched
And landed with an
ACME cartoon cloud.

Then we drove,
Tracks over sand,
To where I shot
And found bodies
Unanimated.

IN THE RUBBLE AT OUR FEET

Their bodies
are as lifeless as the bags
we place them in.

Our enemies,
our kills, abundant
in the rubble at our feet.

Their plans,
their lives, scattered
in the rubble at our feet.

Their kin,
their sons, alongside
in the rubble at our feet.

I AM THE BLOOD

I am the body face down
on the ground to him;
his voice I never heard
ask me if I'm ok, but he did.
His name in my voice
is what woke me
to flames, and I got up
and walked until I bled.
Then I went to the triage,
where I became
the blood
that covered their hands.
They cut off my clothes
and couldn't make it stop,
voices telling me
I'll be ok;
their names
I will never know
because of the morphine
that one shot
into my buttocks
and numbed me
'til I was medevacted
and rode with
a soldier next to me,
with a voice that
I will never hear again
because his name
is now engraved
on a memorial
still being
filled.

BLACKHAWK MEDEVAC

I am strapped down
face down
forced to watch
his face flinch
as my sweat
filters into pain
through the black mesh
gurney
into his eyes
as our wounds ooze
through gauze
saturating
the Blackhawk hull
yearning for
our limbs and
flesh left
behind

DEMEROL DREAMING

LT asks how I'm doin'.
I say, "Good LT, how you doin'?"
He says, "I'm good, how you doin'?"
And I black out before we do it again,
and when we wake, we will do it again;
then she comes in to stick, re-stick, my I.V.,
a beautiful brunette angel of numbness;
I hardly feel the needle go in, and I'm out again,
and I wake up somewhere new,
another tent, and LT's gone; she's gone,
the little fridge with the ice cream sandwiches
is gone, and here comes another angel, petite blonde,
so I'm okay with everything that's gone.
She's come to re-stick my I.V. that dislodged
during the narcotic travels;
"Are you a Combat Lifesaver?" she asks.
"Yes –" I reply.
"So you can help me out a little?" she asks.
I watch each stick—and miss—flinching,
until I turn my arm and expose a solid vein
and the needle strikes it: blood flashes
into the syringe, she stops before she goes too far,
then I'm out again.

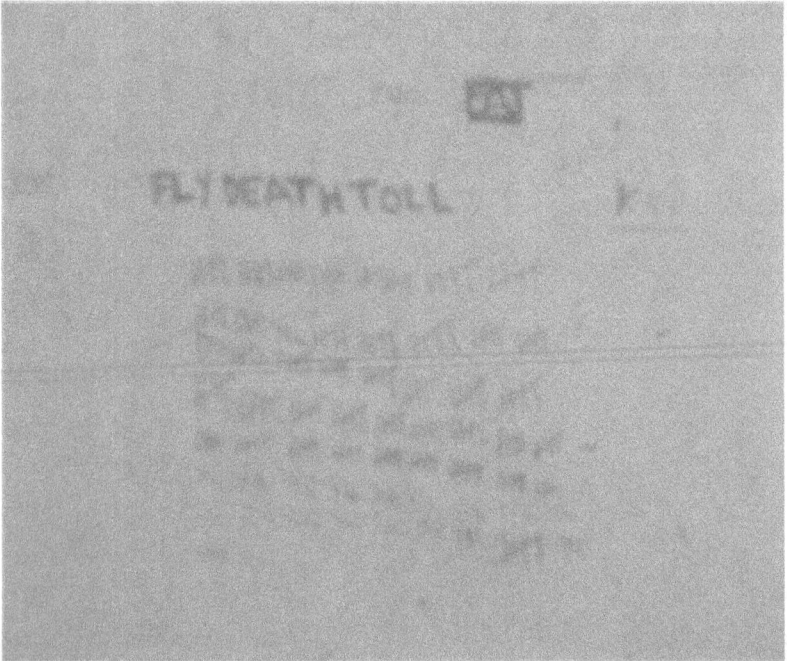

WE CALLED HIM MARTHA STEWART

He was a 6'3" buck sergeant
living in an apartment
blown half to bits,
who touched up the artillery holes
with desert flowers potted
inside chipped terra-cotta.

He made dressers
from discarded MRE boxes
and domesticated a desert dog.

He solved our unit's insect problems
by pulling fish from the Euphrates,
cutting them up
and putting the pieces
into empty water bottles
with tops
cut off,
flipped upside down,
and placed back in.

The rotting meat attracted
the white desert flies and fleas
that could get in but couldn't get out.

NEVER NIGHT

Last night I pulled roving guard.
Tonight I pull radio guard.
Tomorrow night I will pull munitions guard.
Never night will I ever not pull guard.
Never night I dream of every night:
a bed with covers, accompanied by another life.

Every awakening, I battle to hold on
to my never night dream, refusing to return to
a cot with a bag, accompanied by another death,

until my dream becomes my never dream.

No longer does my mind leave its daily nightmare
to the days; now at night, in between guard shifts,
I am still on guard, knowing I or another will die.

GUNPOINT

If you're holding a 50 cal.
Aimed at an Arab,
He'll do anything:
Spin around repeatedly,
Flap his arms like a
Stepped-on lizard.

He'll lift up his Arab dress
And moon you, then turn
Around and show you the front.

You didn't ask
Him to do those things:
Just turn around once with
His arms up before
Coming closer, but

There was a failure
In communication,
So as you watch
And laugh,
The 50 cal. nods
In annoyance.

After some
More squabbling and banter,
He comes forward and
Hands you a note bearing
Your BC's signature saying
He's allowed entrance into camp,
And Mr. 50 cal. will have to wait.

IRAQIS

The turbans atop their heads
serve as dust masks in sandstorms
and face masks and ear muffs
during cold nights;
their sandals shield
their soles from the baking sand
and allow their feet to breath,
but their bodies do little more
than act as rail-thin brass frames
for their dress-like shirts
that slink down
past their shins.

No,
they are not terrorists.
They stare at our convoy,
without food,
without home,
with hollow,
instinctual,
sand-dulled
eyes.

Our commander tells
us humanitarian aide
is behind us;
they will feed them;
our mission is to
liberate them.

So
we stare
at the vehicle
in front of us
as we drive
by them with
our weapons
aimed out
our windows.

71

CNN

I'm lying on the living room floor,
7 years old, at home
watching CNN.

I ask my dad
what the green glowing dots are,
and an RPG hits close;

I'm 19, and CNN is on my windshield;
through NVGs the rounds glow green
down range.

I watch for only a moment
because it's not my shift,
and I fall back to sleep.

A LIGHT

A light, a light
On the horizon.
Do you see it?
        Do I see it?
Like a jammed lighthouse
        Directed
At my location,
Cutting through
The desert fog.
        Is it friendly?
        Should I shoot?
I call it in.
They say,
"Keep an eye
On it."
Then it's gone.
        Where is the light?
Damn.
        Where the Hell is it?
Out.

HERO

Don't think I coulda ever
called Pvt. Sugar hero—
shaking 'im awake for guard
was a bitch.
Sometimes, I swear
he was mumblin' daddy.

You'd wake 'im 10 minutes early
to get his shit on for guard,
and he'd sit right up and talk to you.
You'd finish your shift and damn
if he wasn't back asleep again.

He was good at guardin' his grandma's fudge though
—not even his NCOs got any.
Guarded that fudge better than his cigarettes and dip,
only smoker to bring one carton,
and he couldn't ask Momma for any.

He'd buy smokes 20 bucks a pop,
every once in awhile
he'd pay 10 bucks for a pinch of dip,
depending on how long it'd been.

I got me some of that fudge though,
told 'im I'd leave 'im alone for awhile.
Damn, if it wasn't the best fudge I ever had,
put his grandma in for a medal if I could.

No, I don't think I coulda ever called him hero though,
but he made it home, went straight down to the Dragon's
where even he could buy a beer
and the girls are all high,
so I ain't ever got to.

WE LIE STILL

Zippers rip machinegun tatter
beside our hollow ears
as tan-grained canvas opens
and we are unbirthed
into the backs of deuce-and-a-halfs
and Humvees, thrust in
on black mesh gurneys
by familiar hands;
our red- and blue-threaded
gossamer skin buried
by Army-green wool
which maintains our forms
like upturned indentions
beside newly widowed lovers.

WHAT MAKES THE GREEN GRASS GROW

"What makes the green grass grow?" he asks of me.
The stone-faced sergeant tells the green trainees:
"The blood, the blood of our brave infantry."

"Why is the grass now brown?" he asks Daddy.
"It goes to sleep in autumn just like trees."
"What makes the green grass grow?" he asks of me.

Bullets buzz, Daddy crawls hesitantly.
His buddy's shot, he holds him on his knees.
The blood, the blood of our brave infantry.

"What happens when the brown grass wakes, Daddy?
Will it wake up as green as all the trees?"
"What makes the green grass grow?" he asks of me.

An IED explodes monotony.
Bodies bagged, insurgents just like friendlies.
The blood, the blood of our brave infantry.

"You can't die now, Daddy," a final plea;
"There is so much you never told me, please."
"What makes the green grass grow?" he asks of me.
"The blood, the blood of our brave infantry."

GLOSSARY OF MILITARY TERMS

ATACMS: Army Tactical Missile System – big missiles used for destroying large groups of equipment, buildings, and people.

BC: Battery Commander – an officer who has made the rank of captain and the Army trusts with a battery of his or her own.

Cat-hole: Hole dug for the same purpose that a cat digs a hole.

BDU: Battle Dress Uniform – the everyday uniform of Army soldiers, replaced by the *ACU*, Army Combat Uniform.

DCU: Desert Combat Uniform – tan camouflage with tan suede boots. In 2003, the Army did not have enough of them, so many units deployed to the desert wearing green BDUs and black leather boots.

Deuce-and-a-half: Large, six-wheeled green Army truck that weighs two-and-a-half tons.

E-tool: Entrenching tool – small collapsible shovel that all soldiers carry with them.

FA: Field Artillery – the king of battle. Large metal objects that shoot explosive metal objects in order to destroy other metal objects, buildings, or people.

Five-fifty cord: Green parachute cord rated at five hundred and fifty pounds, often said to hold the entire Army together.

Foxhole: Hole dug from which to guard one's location, also referred to as a grave.

Gator-neck (Neck Gaiter): Neck-warmer that can be pulled over the ears and top of the head.

IED: Improvised Explosive Device or Improved Explosive Device – used by terrorists to kill people.

JLIST: Joint Lightweight Integrated Suit Technology, modern chemical suit.

Kiwi: Brand of shoe polish popular amongst soldiers.

Landstuhl: Location of military base in Germany, where many wounded soldiers are sent for medical care on their way home.

LT: Lieutenant – lowest rank of commissioned officers.

LBE: Load-Bearing Equipment, where ammunition, cards, and snacks are stored.

Medivac: Medical evacuation – occurs after an unpleasant experience; those evacuated are returned home living or dead.

MRE: Meal Ready to Eat – prepackaged soldier food also known as Mr. Es and Mysteries. (They are actually not half bad these days.)

NCO: Noncommissioned Officer – enlisted officer, backbone of the Army.

NBC: Nuclear, Biological, Chemical, scary as Hell.

NVGs: Night Vision Goggles – use small amounts of light and magnify it through a lens, making it possible to see at night and making everything look green.

Pissin' hot: When drugs are found in someone's system during urinalysis screening; often results in the deduction of at least one rank, no matter what rank one is.

Plugger (PLGR): Precision Lightweight GPS Receiver – a great device when used properly, about half the size of a loaf of bread. State-of-the-art 1980's technology.

PT: Physical Training – conducted Monday through Friday at 6:00 am on most military establishments.

RPG: Rocket Propelled Grenade – terrorist Field Artillery.

T-Rat: Tray Rations – Large tins containing food that is warmed up in boiling water to be served in cubes, such as cube of omelet, best with lavish amounts of salt and pepper.

Photograph Acknowledgments

My camera never made it home; however, Jesse Blumenthal and Peter Owens, with whom I served in 2003 during the initial invasion of Iraq, did make it home along with their cameras, and they were generous enough to share their photos in support of *Red Fields*.

Original, color photos can be viewed at JPOUDRIER.COM

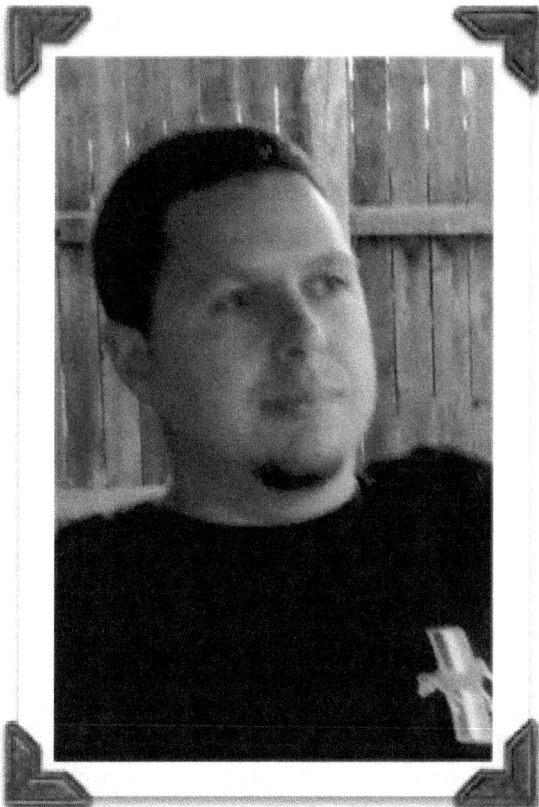

JASON POUDRIER is an Oregon native who currently resides on a small 20-acre ranch in Rush Springs, Oklahoma, with his wife Chelsey. He teaches English at Lawton High School and also coaches Cross Country and Track. He completed his Bachelor's degree in English with an emphasis in creative writing and Master's in Education at Cameron University in 2009. Jason has been invited to read for repeat performances at East Central University's annual Scissortail Creative Writing Festival, in Ada, OK and at Oklahoma LaborFest. An earlier version of *Red Fields* was a semi-finalist in the Blue Lynx Prize competition (Lynx House Press); the poem "High Stakes" was awarded Cameron University's John G. Morris Poetry Prize in 2008, and a version of "High Stakes" was recognized as first place winner by the national Eyes of Babylon poetry contest. Jason has lived in Oklahoma since joining the Army and being stationed at Fort Sill in 2001. In 2003, he was deployed to Iraq, wounded in action, and awarded the Purple Heart. After recovering from his physical wounds, Jason was a member of the Fort Sill Army 10-miler team and was nominated for USO Soldier of the Year; he also competed and was selected twice as 2-14 FA Brigade's NCO of the Quarter. Poudrier advanced to the rank of sergeant before he was honorably discharged.

www.ingramcontent.com/pod-product-compliance
Lightning Source LLC
LaVergne TN
LVHW051605080426
835510LV00020B/3138